BHAKTI YOGA

Yoga for Peace

BHAKTIMEDIA INSPIRED PUBLISHING

Yoga for Peace

There were many contributors to the completion of *"Bhakti Yoga - Yoga for Peace"*, in the form of art, design, editing, advice, layout, proofreading, scriptural research, typing, and typesetting, especially: Sripada Madhava Maharaja, Sripada Tirtha Maharaja, Anita dasi, Bhadra dasi (NZ), Bhanumati dasi, Bhudhara dasa, Brajanath dasa, Hariballabha dasi, Kundalata dasi, Krishna-kamini dasi, Prema-prayojana dasa, Raghava Pandit dasa (Holland), Satya dasi, Syama dasa (UK), Syamarani dasi, Tulasi dasi, Vaijayanti-mala dasi, Vasanti dasi, and The Rays of The Harmonist team.

Special thanks to Isa dasa for archiving all sound files on www.purebhakti.tv

 Gaudiya Vedanta Publications (GVP) is a non-profit publishing group, dedicated to preserving, publishing, and propagating the authentic bhakti yoga teachings of Gaudiya Vaisnavism.

BhaktiMedia provides editorial, design and publication services to promote the bhakti philosophy, arts and culture in every possible way. www.bhaktimedia.org

Books may be purchased in bulk at special discounts for sales promotion, gifts, fundraising, or educational purposes. For details, contact the Sales Department, info@bhaktimedia.org

Artwork of Radha-Krishna on pages **38, 116, 121** copyright © Syamarani dasi. Used with permission.

Photo of Swami BV Narayana on page **69** copyright © Subal Sakha dasa. Used with permission.

Photo of A.C. Bhaktivedanta Swami Prabhupada copyright © Bhaktivedanta Book Trust Intl. Used with permission. www.krishna.com

Translations to verses from the Srimad-Bhagavatam by A.C. Bhaktivedanta Swami Prabhupada © Bhaktivedanta Book Trust Intl. Used with permission.

ISBN: 978-90-817679-1-0

 We print responsibly

First presented on the Gaura Purnima day 8 March, 2012

Yoga for Peace

SRI SRIMAD BHAKTIVEDANTA
NARAYANA GOSVAMI MAHARAJA

BHAKTIMEDIA.ORG

Sri Srimad Bhakti Vedanta
Narayana Gosvami Maharaja

(1921-2010)

Srila BV Narayana Gosvami was a figure of gentle grace and noble learning who inspired in others a desire for self-knowledge and the promise of pure love, divine. He was a master, in every sense, first and foremost of himself and thus by example as much as precept, a master for others. He was humble but strong, especially in his tireless love and compassion for the welfare of others. He was an erudite scholar, but also a self-realised mystic who transcended the limits of the mind and intellect. To meet him was to meet yourself, because in his eyes you could see that he could clearly see you, as you are and for whom you might be. The experience was exciting and transformative. He taught that nothing could replace the living master, yet like masters before him, he wrote scores of volumes. Although he is no longer physically present, with careful reading you might find him looking back at you from these pages and see in that reflection your self, the potential of the realised soul living in a world of ecstatic divine love he described as *Prema Bhakti*.

Read – Discover – Transcend

Dr Michael Geary (*Bhudhara das*)

PUBLISHER'S ACKNOWLEDGMENT

*The publishers gratefully acknowledge the
generous assistance of all the devotees, disciples
and well-wishers of our Gurudeva in the
production of this book.*

Contents

Introduction

Bhakti and *bhakti-yoga* are becoming increasingly popular in *yoga* circles around the world. Although it is easy to recognize the type of *yoga* being practiced by the various poses demonstrated by the practitioner of *hatha-yoga* or one of the many varieties nowadays available, it is not as apparent what exactly *bhakti-yoga* is.

Bhakti-yoga (Sanskrit: भक्ति योग) is one of the types of *yoga* mentioned in Hindu or Vedic philosophy, which represents the spiritual practice of nurturing loving devotion (*bhakti*) to a personal form of God (*bhagavan*).

The *Bhagavad-gita* and *Bhagavata Purana* (known as *Srimad-Bhagavatam*, the ripened fruit of the tree of Vedic literature) are two important scriptures, which explain and develop the attitude of *bhakti*. The *Srimad-Bhagavatam* elucidates the nine-fold practice of *bhakti-yoga* for the *bhakta*, or devotee, which includes hearing its recitation, chanting the verses contained within the *Srimad-Bhagavatam*, and contemplation of the ultimate goal; devotional service to the Divine Couple Sri Sri Radha-Krishna.

"Yoga for Peace" invites the reader to join one of the world's most notable proponents of *bhakti-yoga*, **Sri Srimad Bhaktivedanta Narayana Gosvami Maharaja** (Swami B.V. Narayana), on a journey to discovering pure *bhakti-yoga*, and be inspired by his own exemplary service to, and description of, the sacred path.

Let your journey begin here.

The publishers,

— **BhaktiMedia**

We are fortunate to have His Divine Grace Sri Bhaktivedanta Narayana Maharaja here to help us better understand the yoga path of devotion.

· 1 ·

RADIO INTERVIEW

MAY 23, 2007

Yoga for Peac

Yoga for Peace

The radio host begins the interview:

J ust to introduce myself, I am beginning a radio program here in Houston that is called *"Yoga for Peace."*

What we do is educate people on the vastness of *yoga* and the different paths that one can take in order to reach peace. In this way, people don't get too stuck in the *hatha* or *asana* portion of *yoga*. They will be able to understand that there are other avenues to expand and reach peace. This is what the program is about. We have interviewed *swamis* and other great souls who have come to town, and we play these interviews on the radio so that people can learn.

I will start with an introduction, and then I have a few questions I would like to ask.

There are several paths in *yoga*, and at some point I would like to discuss them all on "Yoga for Peace" Radio. One of those paths is called *bhakti*, or the path of devotion. We are fortunate to have His Divine Grace Sri Bhaktivedanta Narayana Maharaja here to help us better understand this *yogic* path of devotion. Maharaja is a great Vaisnava saint who has circled the globe twenty-five times with his simple message of love and devotion that has attracted the hearts

I don't discriminate between Hindu, Christian, and Buddhist. I know they are all souls within their bodies.

SWAMI BV NARAYANA

SWAMI BV NARAYANA

and souls of millions. At the age of eighty-seven, he is the most revered and eldest of Vaishnava teachers to ever visit the Western world. To date, he has written over fifty books, which have been translated into several languages by his followers. For over half a century, Srila Narayana Maharaja has demonstrated and exemplified the pure life of utter dedication and loving service.

Yoga for Peace

Namaste, Sri Bhaktivedanta Narayana Maharaja. To start, I would like to congratulate you on your title of "**Cultural Ambassador of the City of Houston**," as bestowed by our Mayor to you in the year 2004.

Srila Gurudeva: Oh, thank you.

Radio Host: You're quite welcome. So, to begin, I have a few questions.

Srila Gurudeva: How did she know?

Vishnu dasa (*senior disciple*): There was an article in the newspaper, and we sent some information.

Radio Host: And I read it on the Internet.

Srila Gurudeva: They have also given me American citizenship.

Radio Host: Oh, wonderful! Then you're welcome to come here any time. The door is open. Now, I have some basic questions for you. Why should people practice *yoga*?

Srila Gurudeva: We see that everywhere in this

world – especially in China, Taiwan, and Japan, as well as in other countries – people do physical exercises to keep their bodies strong and durable. It may be that for some time their body can remain like that. They may be strong, with no disease and with some longevity; but one day they must become old, and where will their *yoga* go at that time? They will no longer be able to do exercise. So, for the time being we can exercise to protect our body from disease and make it strong, but this is actually exercise, not *yoga*.

Nowadays, *yoga* is very popular everywhere. The word *yoga* has come from the Indian Sanskrit language. And it means 'joining two things together.' What two things? Most people don't know, but we know, because we practice real *yoga*.

We are not this body. This body is only a bag of urine, blood, stool, and other nasty things, and one day you will have to give it up. But there

There is only
one real language
in the entire
world, and that
is the language
of love.

SWAMI BV NARAYANA

is a soul in this body; you and I are spirit souls. And there is also a Supersoul, the Supreme Lord. Our soul resides in the heart of our body, along with the Supersoul.

By the practice of *bhakti-yoga*, one will know, "I am spirit soul, part and parcel of the Supreme Lord." Then, by love and affection, one comes in touch with Him. Do you understand?

Radio Host: Yes.

Srila Gurudeva: If you want to build a wall, you lay brick after brick, and there must also be some cement. Similarly, if we want to have a connection with the Supreme Lord, there must be *prema*, pure love and affection. By love and affection we can be with Krishna and serve Him. As a result of such service, this body, which is a bag of stool and urine, will be gone forever; and we will realize our very beautiful soul, which is everlasting, with no old age, death, and birth. Then, with our spiritual body, we will serve the beautiful Supreme Lord. This is called *yoga*, and the effect of this *yoga* is that we will no longer have to come to this world to become old and die.

Radio Host: Very good. So the reason to practice *yoga*...

Srila Gurudeva: But one thing - for the time being, we should try to keep our body strong and well, and therefore we should also accept these *yoga* exercises. At the same time, the practice of *bhakti-yoga* is essential. *Bhakti-yoga* is real *yoga*.

Radio Host: In combination with the exercise?

Vishnu dasa: *Hatha-yoga* is for maintaining the body, and *bhakti* is for the soul, for spiritual advancement.

Srila Gurudeva: *Hatha-yoga* is only for the physical body; we are not our bodies.

Radio Host: That leads me to the next question, which you may have already answered in part.

India has many *bhakti-yoga* practitioners. Do you think that *bhakti-yoga* is a practical path for the West?

Srila Gurudeva: Not only for Western countries, but for the whole world. Wherever there are living souls, *bhakti-yoga* is practical.

I've traveled the world about twenty-four times, and in each and every country I go, I preach *bhakti-yoga* and show people by example how to practice it. Thousands upon thousands of persons are accepting the teachings of *bhakti*, and they are now very happy—very happy.

Radio Host: So, it is universal.

Srila Gurudeva: There are millions of devotees who practice *bhakti-yoga*, and I have many thousands of disciples, followers and friends.

Radio Host: Can Christians follow the *bhakti* path and still practice their religion?

Srila Gurudeva: Yes. Actually, Jesus Christ's teaching is very good, and it comes in the

Yoga for Peace

God is very beautiful and is directly perceived by bhakti-yoga.

category of *bhakti-yoga*. But nowadays we see that Christians are not following those teachings.

In the practice of *bhakti-yoga*, pure food is required. We should not take meat, eggs, and wine, and we should not engage in smoking. If we engage in these immoral activities while trying to practice *bhakti-yoga*, that will not be favorable; we will not be able to perform *bhakti-yoga*. But they do not follow this. If they would avoid meat, eggs, smoking, and drinking wine – and at the same time think of the Supreme Lord, who

Bhakti-yoga is the transcendental religion of all souls. It is natural for the soul to serve Krishna. Krishna is love personified.

has a transcendental form, who is very beautiful and merciful, and who is directly perceived by *bhakti-yoga* – then they can practice successfully.

M-E-A-T means 'me eat.' You will be eaten by whoever you are eating; so don't eat meat. A child in the womb comes from an egg. If you eat eggs, you are doing so against the will of the Supreme Lord. He has not created these beings to be eaten. For your eating He has created milk, sugar, ghee, so many fruits, vegetables, curd, and unlimited other edibles.

Radio Host: How do you feel about the poor treatment of cows in this country in order to extract their milk? Do you feel that such milk is still pure?

Srila Gurudeva: That is a very wrong thing. It is cruelty. The Supreme Lord will surely punish such cruel persons. They will take birth as cows, and those cows will take birth as humans and do the same thing to them. All activities have a reaction

– good or bad – so we should not do such things.

Radio Host: We should avoid the milk that is in the grocery stores? Is that what you are saying?

Srila Gurudeva: It is like meat. We should not take it.

Radio Host: I very much agree. You have answered a lot of my questions.

Brajanath dasa (*senior disciple & secretary*): Gurudeva, there are also cows that are treated well, and fed an organic diet.

Srila Gurudeva: This is good. I have seen this in Holland; millions of cows – very big cows. We can take the milk of such cows.

Radio Host: Unless a person can go and see how the cows are treated in this country and many other places, it is difficult to know. Their saying it is organic does not mean that the cows are treated well. It just means they are fed different food.

Srila Gurudeva: We have many cows in our Ashram (monastery). We give proper care and food to them. First they give milk to their calves;

only then do we take their milk.

Radio Host: How can *bhakti-yoga* contribute to peace – personally and globally?

Srila Gurudeva: *Bhakti-yoga* is the transcendental religion of all souls. It is natural for the soul to serve Krishna. Krishna is the Supreme Lord. God is love, and love is God. Krishna is love personified. If anyone serves Him, that person becomes fully happy with pure love and affection. He is never unhappy, because in the transcendental

The devotee prays, "O God, You are so merciful. Please be merciful to me."

world there are no diseases or old age, and no problem exists of any kind. There is only happiness, and more happiness; so that person will be eternally happy.

Bhakti-yoga is very easy to follow. The devotee prays, "O God, You are extremely merciful. Please be merciful to me." And he chants the Lord's names.

The names of the Supreme Lord are very powerful. In a moment the Lord can create millions of universes, and again in a moment He can destroy them, and then re-create them. He is causelessly merciful. He has all good qualities. He has invested all His power, all His mercy, and all His qualities in His names, and that is why His names are so powerful. We chant and meditate upon His names: *Hare Krishna, Hare Krishna, Krishna Krishna, Hare Hare — Hare Rama, Hare Rama, Rama Rama, Hare Hare.*

Whatever language we speak, whether we live

in Western or Eastern countries, we can very easily chant and offer respectful obeisances to Him. We can very easily become situated in *bhakti-yoga*, and thus become liberated from this world and be happy forever.

Radio Host: Can one chant Jesus's name and have the same effect as chanting Krishna's name?

Srila Gurudeva: Jesus is not God, the Supreme Lord. He is the Son of God. The Father has a form, because in the first chapter of the Bible, it is written that God created man after His own image. If God has no image, how can He create the human form, or human image? God has form and so many qualities. All qualities reside in Him.

Brajanath dasa: Other names can also be meditated upon?

Srila Gurudeva: What names do Christians have for God?

Brajanath dasa: Jehovah, Yahweh.

Yoga for Peace

Srila Gurudeva: The name Christ came when the young Jesus went to India, to all our sacred places. In Vrindavan, where we come from, he heard the name of Krishna, the Supreme Lord, and saw His form. Then he went to South India, where they pronounce Krishna as "*Krushna*." From Krushna came Krista, and from Krista came Christ. Christ is the same as Krishna, and therefore we can chant the name Christ, or Jehovah, or whatever name you wish.

Radio Host: Allah?

Srila Gurudeva: Allah refers to *brahma* (Supreme Being). Allah means 'there is nothing greater than that,' and therefore He is Allah, or *brahma*; He is the greatest. But one thing: we say that God is Bhagavan (full with six opulences, namely wealth, fame, knowledge, strength, beauty, and renunciation). *Brahma* has no form or qualities. It is merely the effulgence of the nails of the Lord. As the sunrays and light have no form, so *brahma* and Allah are like the effulgence of Bhagavan. But Bhagavan has form and all qualities, and He is very merciful.

Radio Host: That is how peace can come globally – when everyone realizes that it is all the same?

Srila Gurudeva: By this we can always be peaceful; not quarreling and not slaughtering animals. Animals are also souls, just as we are souls. By this awareness we can be happy.

Radio Host: That sounds good to me. Another question: Do you believe the *bhakti* practice has contributed to your good health and longevity?

Srila Gurudeva: That may be. I am always happy, traveling the entire world, writing so many books, and preaching *bhakti-yoga* everywhere. I have no worldly desires; I have given them up forever. Actually, I have no home, but everywhere is my home. I have no wife, but I have millions of daughters and sons.

Q: How can one find his true teacher?

Radio Host: Yes, a very loving family.

Srila Gurudeva: I don't discriminate between Hindu, Christian, and Buddhist. I know they are all souls within their bodies – sons and daughters of God.

Radio Host: One more question: How can one find his true teacher?

Srila Gurudeva: It is very rare – very rare – to find such a teacher, or *guru*.

To become happy, one should not give pain to any living entity.

There are some symptoms by which he is recognized. He should know all the Vedic literature. He should be so expert that he can remove the doubts of his disciples. A *guru* should have realization of God so that he can give God from his heart to others' hearts. Next, he should be detached from worldly desires.

Such a *guru* is very rare. However, if you pray to God with a clean and simple heart, "O God, You are merciful. Please arrange that I can meet such a *guru*," He will somehow mercifully arrange that such a *guru* will come to your door and teach you everything.

Radio Host: So the key is to be pure of heart in one's desire. Very good. Well, I don't want to keep you very long. I've kept you a long time already. I just want to go ahead and ask if you have a final message to give to the listeners of the radio program.

Srila Gurudeva: If any person wants to be happy, he must follow *bhakti-yoga*. Without chanting the name of the Supreme Lord, one can never be happy; never, never. To chant the name properly he should give up eating meat and eggs, drinking wine, smoking, and other bad habits. He should not harm animals. He should not give any pain

Sarve sukhino bhavantu; I pray to the Lord that all should be happy.

to animals, or to any living entities. Thus, he can become happy. This is my final message. Also, I pray to the Lord that all should be happy - *sarve sukhino bhavantu*. All should be without disease.

I also pray that you will personally be happy in your life and realize God.

Radio Host: It seems you have taught your disciples very well, because they can fill in your sentences for you.

Srila Gurudeva: They are very expert. I am now eighty-seven years old. They have taken care of me in such a way that I can travel and write.

Radio Host: Are you going to continue to travel?

Sripad Madhava Maharaja (*senior disciple & personal attendant*)**:** Yes, certainly.

Srila Gurudeva: If I am a citizen in India, and here also, I will have to come.

Radio Host: It has been a wonderful, wonderful pleasure meeting you. Thank you so much. It has been a great honor to meet you. I really appreciate this time that you have given me, and I hope this message can get out to others.

Namaste

"There is only one
religion, and that natural
religion is love."

ROOM CONVERSATION

JUNE 8, 1998

· 2 ·

God, Love &
Reincarnatio

God, Love & Reincarnation

*Sri Srimad Narayana Gosvami Maharaja
(Srila Gurudeva) speaks to an elderly female guest in a
room conversation that took place in Los Angeles,
California on June 8th, 1998:*

Srila Gurudeva: Do you want to ask me any
questions?

Guest: What organization do you represent?

Srila Gurudeva: Bhudhara prabhu, my disciple,
can answer this.

Bhudhara dasa: There is very little organization

actually. This is all happening by God's grace. This is Srila Bhaktivedanta Narayana Gosvami Maharaja. He is a teacher and a *guru*, and he lives in Mathura, India. He is a scholar and a writer, and he gives lectures. Many people come and listen to him talk about God - high topics about God. He talks about how one can develop love and affection for God, and love and affection for our fellow man. He talks about how to live in peace and harmony, and eventually, at the end of this life, go back to God.

He has come to America, and we have been taking him from city to city. We have been in Washington, New York, Houston, and now Los Angeles; and after this we are going to San Francisco. We are inviting people to come and have some exchange with him, to ask him questions, and to learn about this science called Krishna consciousness. Have you heard about Hare Krishna?

Hare Krishna
Hare Krishna
Krishna Krishna
Hare Hare

Hare Rama
Hare Rama
Rama Rama
Hare Hare

HARE KRISHNA MAHA-MANTRA

God, Love & Reincarnation

Guest: Yes, I think I was in a place like this some years back. His picture was on the wall.

Devotee: You've seen pictures of Krishna?

Guest: There were flowers, fruits, and a handkerchief on the altar. Do you know the symbolic meaning of this?

Bhudhara dasa: These are simple offerings of love. In the *Bhagavad-gita*, Krishna says, "If you offer Me something with love and devotion, like a flower, some vegetable, or some fruit or water, I will accept it."

Srila Gurudeva: We see that there is no difference between God and Krishna. It's the same idea. Krishna is very merciful. If you pray to Him and glorify Him by any song, or by any words, He will hear and He will be pleased. You can pray, "Oh God, You are so merciful." (Srila Gurudeva sings, and devotees join in): *Hare Krishna, Hare Krishna, Krishna Krishna, Hare Hare — Hare Rama, Hare Rama, Rama Rama, Hare Hare.*

This means, "O Supreme Personality of God-head, You are so merciful. You have given me this human body, intelligence, a heart so soft and full of love and affection. I want to serve You eternally, so please be merciful to me."
(Srila Gurudeva sings again, and devotees join in): *"Govinda Damodara Madhaveti, Govinda Damodara Madhaveti; Govinda Damodara Madhaveti, Govinda Damodara Madhaveti."*

Srila Gurudeva: When we are dying, when we are on our death-bed, there is no one to help us. We are not even able to take a breath. We are full of mucus and we want to take a breath, but we cannot. We want to move our hands from here to there, but we cannot do so. We cannot do anything. At that time we pray, "Oh God, You are so merciful. Be pleased with me; sprinkle Your mercy upon me. Take me to Your eternal abode, where I will serve You."

God, Love & Reincarnation

We want to be free from becoming old and again taking birth in this miserable world. There is so much pain at the time of birth, and there is so much pain at the time of death; so we must pray to God. He is everywhere. He is in everyone and in every atom of the world. He hears whatever you utter. When you weep and sing and glorify Him, He will at once hear you and come to you and liberate you forever.

We never pray to Krishna, the Supreme Personality of Godhead: "God, give me bread and butter." Rather, we want to serve Him with bread and butter. We want that this chain of birth and death and suffering will be stopped forever.

This body is not my 'self'

This body is not my 'self'. It is something like a garment. The body is covered with a garment, and it is also like a garment. One day, when we become old, we will have to give up this garment. Surely, we will have to do so.

What is God? What is the soul? You can realize this only in this human body; otherwise it is not possible. If you are an animal, a tree, a creeper, or an insect, you cannot realize this; you cannot understand all these truths. You can understand something only in this human body. You have some intelligence given by the Lord, so try to use it.

God, Love & Reincarnation

There is only one religion. That religion is natural, and that natural religion is love and affection for God and for everyone.

Also, don't kill animals and eat their flesh and eggs. If you do, your mind and heart will become like them. If you eat the flesh of hogs and pigs, your mentality and heart will become like them. Your nature will be changed to be like them. What is the meaning of meat? ME-EAT. If you eat meat, that animal will come as a human and eat you. So don't take meat, eggs, and other bad things. God has given fruits, milk, butter, curd, and so many other nice foodstuffs. Personally, I have never taken meat, eggs, or wine in my entire life.

If you want to be pure to serve God, then

All the names of Krishna are the embodiment of love.

If you are in touch with that love, your life will be happy!

you must follow this. There is only one religion. That religion is natural, and that natural religion is love and affection for God and for everyone. Even a dog, a lion, a bear, and a tiger have love for their wife and children. Although they may eat the flesh of others, they have love for their families. To love is natural for all. Trees also love; they want to love each other. How? Little creepers love trees and embrace them.

If you touch a tree's leaf as though caressing it, the tree will be very happy. If you take a knife to cut the branches, the tree will be scared. It will tremble. If you tell a dog, "Come on, come on," he will come. And if you are mean, then the dog will attack you. So, our nature – the nature of the soul – is love.

We should practice this. We should love our mother and father, for they have done so many things for us. We should love our wife and children; not divorcing each other twenty or thirty times.

Krishna is very charming & beautiful. He is the embodiment of love.

If you have love, it may be gradually transferred to God. If you have no love and you are always quarreling, you cannot have the mercy of God. We should try to discover this love in our heart, and try to practice chanting the holy names: "*Hare Krishna, Hare Krishna, Krishna Krishna, Hare Hare — Hare Rama, Hare Rama, Rama Rama, Hare Hare.*"

All the names of Krishna are the embodiment of love. '*Hare*' is the embodiment of love. '*Krishna*' is very charming and beautiful, and He is the embodiment of love. '*Rama*' is the embodiment of love. If you are in touch with this love, your life will be happy; otherwise it is not possible. If a man is always cruel to others, he cannot be happy.

I do not have to die, and I will teach you a trick so that you will also not die.

Guest: Do you believe in reincarnation?

Srila Gurudeva: We see that two children take birth at exactly the same time, but one has no backbone, no intelligence, and eyes that cannot see. The other child is born as the son of President Clinton or a very rich person. Why are there such differences? In India, and also in Western countries, some people remember their past life. There are many examples of this.

So, we believe in reincarnation. If you don't believe in this, all your ideas will be illogical. Why is one person very intelligent, and why is one so unintelligent that he is like a donkey? Why is one person very beautiful and one is not beautiful at all? The philosophy of reincarnation answers these questions. There are so many reasons to believe this.

Devotee: Couldn't you say that because the father or mother are beautiful, the child will be beautiful?

Srila Gurudeva: We see many fathers and mothers who are very beautiful, but their sons or daughters have crooked teeth, or ugly faces, or no bones, or eyes that cannot see. The soul is immortal, but he has adopted this material position by forgetting God and by the subsequent touch of *maya*, illusion.

Why is a person in jail? He has done something wrong. Similarly, we are now in jail – the jail of the deluding energy called *maya*. We are being crushed by *maya*.

If you realize this fact, you will at once pray to God, "Save me. Save me." Have you heard of the Vedas? They are very old scriptures. These facts are written in the Vedic scriptures, and we realize this.

Srila Gurudeva: Is my mother hearing all these things? You are like my mother.

Guest: I am like your mother? Yes, I hear you. I had a surgery some years ago. Do you know medical terms?

Bhudhara dasa: No, he is a doctor of the soul, not the body.

Srila Gurudeva: I had surgery too, so you are like me. You are my mother – the son and mother both had surgery.

God, Love & Reincarnation

43

Guest: Do you have a living mother?

Srila Gurudeva: That mother has left this world, but there are so many mothers. I think that this young lady is also my mother, and you are too. All ladies are my mother. We think like this in India.

Guest: I am glad to have such a gracious son.

Srila Gurudeva: Our relation should be eternal.

Guest: So we never die?

Srila Gurudeva: No, I do not have to die, and I will teach you a trick so that you will also not die.

Guest: What happens to those who die? What happens to their soul?

Srila Gurudeva: They will take birth again. According to their activities in this life, a person will have to reap the fruits of those activities in their future birth.

Guest: So we should go to the cemetery and pray to God to take their soul in His possession?

Srila Gurudeva: Yes, we want this. We are trying

to help everyone, and that is why we perform *kirtan*, congregational chanting of the holy name and fame of Krishna. We chant *"Hare Krishna"* so that even trees, animals, dogs, and even any person who doesn't want to hear, can receive spiritual benefit. We chant *"Hare Krishna"* very loudly, so that the transcendental sound vibration will go everywhere. And we widely distribute *prasadam*, remnants of sacred foods offered to God. This will help them.

God created man in
His own image, in the image
of God He created him; male
and female He created them.

GENESIS 1:27

· 3 ·

In His
Own Image

In His Own Image

I have come from a very faraway holy place in India, called Vrindavan, to share something with you. We all desire happiness and peace of mind. No one wants difficulties, sorrows and suffering. Even a tiny ant, or monkeys, dogs, and hogs, all want happiness. But how can we attain happiness? This is the question.

We ask Buddhists that if we are 'zero', where has this world originated from?

In His Own Image

Nowadays there are so many religious movements and missionaries, including Buddhism, Christianity, Muslims, and the followers of Sanatana Dharma, Hindus. We all want happiness. And we see that all of them present their own special theories. Nowadays Buddhism is being preached everywhere in India, as well as in China and everywhere else in the world. They say, "You should follow us, and we will give you happiness. This world is void. Everything has been created from 'zero', and in the end everything will return to being zero."

But we ask them that if we are zero, where has this world originated from? And why do we desire happiness? Where have all the different species of life in this world come from? We see so many different kinds of humans, trees, creepers and animals, but where have they come from if everything is zero? We ask the Buddhists, "What is the need of your preaching if the whole world is zero? Who are you preaching to if they are all zero? How can you preach to zero?" This is very strange and wonderous. If everything is zero, then how can they give any happiness to others? Thus, it is evident that they cannot give pleasure, happiness, and peace of mind.

They cite this example of how to attain happiness: A Buddhist *guru*, at the age of eighty, lived in a very deep cave inside a mountain. Upon entering the cave, the *guru* told his disciples to place a very heavy stone at the mouth of that cave. As there was no food, no air, no water, or anything in the cave, he slowly began to die inside. He became so weak that he was not able to open the mouth of that cave, and finally he died. They call this *nirvana* and claim that he attained happiness. But we should be very cautious of this.

Also we see that Christians speak of a God. They want bread and butter from God. "Oh, God, please give me butter and bread; daily bread and

In His Own Image

everything." But they maintain the idea that God has no shape, no attributes, no qualities; nothing. If God is formless, then how can He be so merciful? However, in their religious book, the Bible, in Genesis it has been stated, "God created man after His own image." So God has a form, and from His form, He has created us human persons. I don't know why they don't acknowledge this fact, even though it is written in the Bible.

There you can read that God does have shape.

G-O-D. Three letters. "G" is for Generator of this world; He has generated this world, and is the creator of this world. "O" is for Operator. Who operates this world? So many persons take birth and so many are dying; some are wealthy, others are poor; some are blind, while others have eyes. But who manages this world? Who gives us intelligence, and who gives us this body? There is someone who controls everything.

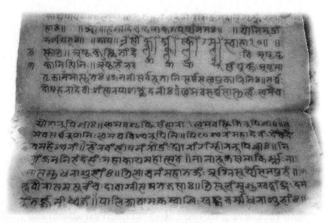

The ancient Vedas, arising from India's cradle of Wisdom

In His Own Image

And "D" is for Destroyer. How can a form-less person with no power or attributes, perform all these activities? There must be a Supreme Personality controlling the whole universe, a Supreme Personality of Godhead, who possesses a very beautiful form. If God is shapeless, and has no mercy, then where has this world origi-nated from? Nothing can be created from zero. There must be something, a source, from which everything is created. In the Vedas (*Sri Isopanisad*, Invocation) it is stated:

> *oṁ pūrṇam adaḥ pūrṇam idaṁ*
> *pūrṇāt pūrṇam udacyate*
> *pūrṇasya pūrṇam ādāya*
> *pūrṇam evāvaśiṣyate*

"The Personality of Godhead is perfect and complete, and because He is completely perfect, all emanations from Him, such as this phenom-enal world, are perfectly equipped as complete wholes. Whatever is produced of the Complete Whole is also complete in itself. Because He is the Complete Whole, even though so many complete units emanate from Him, He remains the complete balance." (Translation by A.C. Bhaktivedanta Swami Prabhupada)

God is *akhanda*, complete, and we are all eternal servants of that Supreme Personality of Godhead. He is so beautiful; bent in three places He stands, playing on His flute. Being ever-youthful, He charms the whole world, including the creepers, trees, and animals.

He has created us humans, so very beautiful. Just see how beautiful you are. So He is very charming and attractive, and that is why He is called "Krishna". You may also call Him Christ. There is no harm in that, because the word Christ has come from Krishna. We have a history that Jesus traveled to India and visited Vrindavan (the birthplace of Krishna). When Jesus continued on to Jagannatha Puri, He saw that attractive Krishna and became a very pure devotee, like a son. At last He arrived in Jerusalem, from where He preached. In India, Krishna is also called 'Krista'. Krista became 'Khristos' in Greek, and from that the name Jesus 'Christ' is derived. So we also accept that Christ is the embodiment of wholesale love and affection, and that Krishna is truly the Supreme Personality of Godhead — very beautiful and attractive, possessing all qualities. He has created this world and it is He who manages everything.

فَاطِرُ السَّمَوَاتِ وَالْأَرْضِ ۚ جَعَلَ لَكُمْ مِنْ أَنْفُسِكُمْ أَزْوَاجًا وَمِنَ الْأَنْعَامِ أَزْوَاجًا ۚ يَذْرَؤُكُمْ فِيهِ ۚ لَيْسَ كَمِثْلِهِ شَيْءٌ ۚ وَهُوَ السَّمِيعُ الْبَصِيرُ ﴿١١﴾

The same has been stated in the scriptures of Mohammedans. Although they don't acknowledge that Khuda (the Almighty God and the Loving Creator) or Allah has a form, they do accept that Khuda or Allah is the Supreme Personality of Godhead. It has been written in their own Koran: '*innallaha khalaqa adama ala suratihi*' — Allah or Khuda has created all human beings in His own image. So all scriptures say the same thing. Our Vedas say that Krishna is very beautiful in His young age, and He will always remain young throughout the three phases of time (past, present and future).

Somehow we have forgotten this, but if we contemplate His names, we will be liberated and become happy forever. Krishna has invested all His powers, all His mercy, and all His attributes in His names. What are these names?

Hare Krishna, Hare Krishna, Krishna Krishna, Hare Hare — Hare Rama, Hare Rama, Rama Rama, Hare Hare.

By chanting these names regularly, even for just ten days, while giving up your bad habits like

God is very charming and attractive — that is why He is called "Krishna".

eating meat, eggs, and drinking wine — by following this pure process — I guarantee that you will be happy forever.

Nityananda Prabhu has personally guaranteed: "You will be happy, you will be happy, you will be happy!" Today I have explained briefly that you will become happy by chanting *Hare Krishna, Hare Krishna, Krishna Krishna, Hare Hare — Hare Rama, Hare Rama, Rama Rama, Hare Hare.* If you come again tomorrow and bring your friends and colleagues, I will explain more.

*" These holy names
will inspire and purify all living
beings, whether they are
aware or not."*

FESTIVAL, ODESSA

MAY 29, 2002

· 4 ·

Mantra of Divine Love

Mantra of Divine Love

Water, air and practically everything is polluted these days. As the oceans are polluted by poisons, thus poisoning both the fish and the fish eaters, material sound vibration also pollutes and poisons the atmosphere. People spray poisons to kill insects, thus poisoning the grains and those who eat them. Similarly, material sound vibration in the form of abuses, criticism of others, quarreling and so forth, and in fact any material vibration, pollutes the minds, senses and hearts of everyone throughout the world. We can counteract this pollution and pain by chanting the Hare Krishna mantra.

An example may be given of a big pond. If you take a stone and throw it into a pond, the waves that are created will touch all edges of the pond. This universe is like that pond. Chanting *Hare Krishna, Hare Krishna, Krishna Krishna, Hare Hare — Hare Rama, Hare Rama, Rama Rama, Hare Hare,* creates many waves of spiritual vibration. Those waves touch everything – up to the end of the world – moving here and there and purifying the entire universe from all pollution.

Hare Krishna
Hare Krishna
Krishna Krishna
Hare Hare

Hare Rama
Hare Rama
Rama Rama
Hare Hare

HARE KRISHNA MAHA-MANTRA

A Japa Mala is used to repeat the mantra

Lord Krishna is inconceivably powerful. He can create the entire universe in a second and then destroy it, and again He can create many worlds. He has invested all His mercy, power and opulence in His names, and thus they are also unlimitedly powerful. They very quickly travel throughout the universe as spiritual sound vibrations, and the pollution gradually disappears.

These holy names will inspire and purify all living beings, whether they are aware or not.

Trees, creepers, animals and insects cannot speak. They cannot understand our language. Still, everyone – not only humans, but all creatures throughout this universe – will be touched by the powerful holy name, whether they are aware of it or not. If one touches fire knowingly or unknowingly, he will feel its effects. Similarly, these holy names will inspire and purify all living beings, whether they are aware or not. Trees, grasses and humans all become fortunate when they hear about Krishna, and even the creatures in the jungles are gradually liberated from suffering.

If we chant loudly, all our senses will be purified, and there will be nothing to criticize and no unhappy memories. By material endeavors we cannot control the unhappy and unbeneficial thoughts that enter our minds, but they are conquered very easily by chanting. Gradually our hearts will be cleansed by such chanting, and then we will realize that our real self-interest – the Soul of our souls – is Lord Krishna. Therefore, if we serve Him, we and the entire world are benefited.

"God is Love and Love is God"
Chant Hare Krishna and Be Happy!

*"God is Love
and Love is God"*

*Chant
Hare Krishna and
Be Happy!*

"I became detached from this world... and began thinking that I must go to a realized holy master who can teach me."

INTERVIEW

DECEMBER 23, 1998

· 5 ·

Interview by a Reporter

Interview by a Reporter

Reporter: How many followers do you have, of *bhakti-yoga*?

Srila Gurudeva: In the entire world?

Reporter: Yes.

Srila Gurudeva: There may be hundreds of thousands.

Reporter: In the information I received about you, it said that you were born in a priestly family. Have you inherited your position by birth, or did you choose to study this?

Srila Gurudeva: In India, *brahmanas* are often seen in very aristocratic families. They are learned and also wealthy. I was in that type of family.

Reporter: When did you start studying *bhakti-yoga*?

Srila Gurudeva: I have been chanting and remembering Krishna since my birth. My father was a devotee and my mother was also a devotee. Born in a devotee family, I was a devotee from the beginning.

Reporter: Can you describe what you have gone through since you were young – what you had to do and the various stages you had to go through – to get to where you are now?

Interview by a Reporter

Srila Gurudeva

SWAMI BV NARAYANA

From my early childhood, I was very fond of reading and studying the Vedas.

Srila Gurudeva: I used to rise early in the morning, at about 4am, and I would chant and remember: "*Hare Krishna, Hare Krishna, Krishna Krishna, Hare Hare — Hare Rama, Hare Rama, Rama Rama, Hare Hare.*" I was always worshiping Lord Krishna and Lord Rama. I was always very kind to all animals, trees, creepers, and grasses. From the beginning of my childhood, I was very fond of reading and studying the Vedas,

Interview by a Reporter

Upanisads, Ramayana, and Mahabharata. I was always a very religious person, with a great taste for studying.

I was also a good soccer player. In track and field I participated in the high jump, long jump, and the 440-yard, 880-yard, 1 mile, 2 mile, and up to 5 mile race. There are 1760 yards in one mile, so 440 yards = quarter mile race, and 880 yards = half mile race. In the entire district of India where I lived, no one was equal to me in this. I also used to sail boats, cycle, and play other sports also.

When I used to compete in athletics, thousands of people in the audience would clap, and for that reason I was selected for a high-ranking position in the police force.

Reporter: So you were a policeman before?

Srila Gurudeva: Yes. All high-rank police officers were pleased with me because of my good character. I never took a bribe from anyone – not a

"My Guru Maharaja"

single penny. As you may know, India is very famous for bribery and other types of corruption, but I was always so honest that everyone loved me. I was chosen for a promotion by the police officers, but at that time I met my Guru Maharaja, my spiritual master, and I became totally renounced.

Interview by a Reporter

Here is the history of how I met my Guru Maharaja. I was seeing that no one can be happy in this world without transcendental life. I saw that although there is beauty in this world, it lasts only for a moment. There is love and affection, but with self-interest. No one here can love purely because everyone wants their own self-interests fulfilled.

I understood that neither wealth nor praise can give happiness, and that everyone is bound to become old and die. I considered that I am not this body. I am actually inside the body, captured there.

Who am I, and who is controlling this world? Where did this world come from? Who is God – G-O-D – the Generator, Operator, and Destroyer of this world? I began to think about all this, and I became detached from this world. I began thinking that I must go to a realized holy master who can teach me.

"I went to the Himalayas
and searched all over
India, but ...

SWAMI BV NARAYANA

I did not find the type of Guru I was looking for."

Reporter: So who did you go to?

Srila Gurudeva: I went to the Himalayas and other places. I searched all over India, but I did not find the type of Guru I was looking for. Then, one day while I was in my service as a police officer, a disciple of my Gurudeva came to my town. He spoke with me and convinced me to come to Navadvipa, in West Bengal where I met Gurudeva and heard him speak at a *Bhagavat-sapta* (Seven-day discourse on the entire

Srimad-Bhagavatam). I was fully satisfied by his words, and I vowed that I would go to serve him and learn all transcendental topics from him. I quickly left my service at the police force, although the police and my family were not in a mood to let me go.

Reporter: And your family?

Srila Gurudeva: I was married and had children, but I was detached. I forgot everything of this world and was only thinking, "Where is Krishna, where is Krishna? How can I serve Him? I want to serve Him. I want to see Him." I quickly left everything and came to join our Gurudeva's mission, and gradually I began to learn all transcendental truths.

Who is God? He is the embodiment of love and affection. He is Krishna, the Supreme Personality of Godhead. He has so much love, and He has a very beautiful body. All other beautiful bodies have come from Him, and all pure love has come from Him. When I heard this, I fully surrendered and Gurudeva gave me initiation. I began to serve him in all ways, with all my energy. I used to cook for him.

Reporter: How old were you when you did this?

Srila Gurudeva: My age was 24 or 25.

Reporter: Sorry, keep going. I will have to interrupt from time to time.

Brajanath dasa: You were cooking for him...

Srila Gurudeva: I used to wash his clothes, and I used to take dictations from him for his magazine articles. When he spoke on any subject, I would hear very attentively and note down his words in my heart. I used my "heart-camera" to note it all down – not a tape recorder. I never used tape recorders.

Reporter: It is cheating, isn't it? And I use the computer as well.

Srila Gurudeva: I never believed in computers and tape recorders; they can cheat us. I always used my heart.

My taste in all devotional services, beginning with chanting and remembering, gradually increased more and more. I gradually began to learn the Vedas, Upanisads, Srimad-Bhagavatam, and other books more deeply, and I began to realize all transcendental truths.

Guru Maharaja ordered me to write some books and to translate books from Bengali to Hindi. He put me in charge of a preaching center, and he made me editor of a magazine called *Sri Bhagavata Patrika*. I then began to translate many Bengali books to Hindi. My Guru Maharaja was so happy with me for this, and he sent me to preach in various places. He created the Gaudiya Vedanta Society to preach throughout the world. He also gave *sannyasa* (the renounced order) to a very famous preacher from India. That preacher's name is Srila Bhaktivedanta Swami Maharaja, and his disciples also call him

Prabhupada. He established ISKCON (International Society for Krishna Consciousness) centers all over the world, including here in Australia as well as in America and England. He took *sannyasa* in Mathura from my Guru-deva, and I was present there and served him. He made devotees all over the world, and he told me to come and help them.

I have come here as a preacher of ancient Indian and Vedic culture, to teach bhakti-yoga.

Interview by a Reporter

A.C. Bhaktivedanta Swami

I have come here as a preacher of ancient Indian culture and Vedic culture, to preach *hari-nama* (the pure chanting of the holy names of Sri Krishna) and *bhakti-yoga*. I am now preaching throughout the world, and this is my sixth world tour.

Reporter: Sixth world tour? I'm jealous.

Srila Gurudeva: Everywhere I go, so many persons develop love for me. They also worship me, but I see them as my friends, and I think, "I must help them". I am concerned about their happiness, and I want to help them so that they will not become old at any time.

As you know, the president of America had such a high position, but he could not control his senses. He was attached to his office girl. This shows that he was not happy.

In this world, people cannot control their senses. They cannot control their future situations so that they will never become old. Also, they cannot control their suffering and sorrows, and so many problems. You may be very beautiful at present, but one day your teeth will fall out.

Reporter: Thank you for reminding me.

Srila Gurudeva: Your hair will become white, and it may be that your eyes will become very weak.

Interview by a Reporter

There is no birth or death for the soul, so why are we suffering?

Reporter: I wear glasses already.

Srila Gurudeva: The day will come when you will not be able to walk without the help of a cane. And one day, although you will not want to do so, you will have to give up this body.

There is no birth or death for the soul, so why are we coming here and suffering? It is because we have forgotten our loving father, mother, friend, and most beloved – Krishna, the embodiment of love. We are His parts and parcels, but now we have forgotten Him; that is why we experience

When a soul is connected with God, that is pure yoga – bhakti-yoga.

birth, old age, death, and their concomitant sufferings. One day we were little babies, and one day, although we desire that this stage will not come, we will all have to give up these bodies.

We can stop all of these things very easily by chanting and remembering Sri Krishna. Anyone – old, young, Hindu, or Muslim – anyone can chant the name of God. There is no time limit;

Interview by a Reporter

you can do this in the night or the day. And there is no expense at all. Without any money or any special conditions, we can chant, "*Hare Krishna Hare Krishna, Krishna Krishna, Hare Hare — Hare Rama, Hare Rama, Rama Rama, Hare Hare.*" By this chanting, you will develop love for all. You will not be able to kill any animal, or even a tree. You will not want to give pain even to grass. You will see God and souls everywhere. God is so merciful. This is our mission.

Reporter: This may be a stupid question, but you are obviously vegetarian?

Srila Gurudeva: Yes. If anyone is vegetarian, then he will surely be very kind to all. Do you know the meaning of meat?

Reporter: Well, it is an animal that you are killing to feed yourself, isn't it?

Srila Gurudeva: Meat: M-E-A-T divides into two sections—ME-EAT. Whom I will eat will eat me after some days. The animals we eat will later get human bodies and eat us (at that time we will have animal bodies). So we should not eat meat.

Reporter: We should just leave it?

Srila Gurudeva: Yes. This is called *bhakti-yoga*. What is the meaning of *yoga*? If there are two or more things and we combine them or join them together, this is *yoga*. 1+1 equals 2 – this is *yoga*. When a soul is connected with God, this is pure *yoga* – *bhakti-yoga*. If we want to connect two bricks, we must bring some ingredient that will connect them, like mud or cement, and then they will be connected. If one wants to connect souls with God, there must be something added to bond them. What is that? It is love and affection.

If we have love and affection for you, you will have love and affection for us. In this world everything is bound by love and affection, but here it is not pure. For example, after some time, husbands and wives divorce each other.

Interview by a Reporter

*All souls have love and affection
— even trees have it*

Interview by a Reporter

In the spiritual world, however, love and affection is so pure that the soul can be connected with God forever, eternally and transcendentally; this is called *bhakti-yoga*. I have love and affection here in my heart, and you have it also. All souls have affection and love, and even trees have it. If trees do not meet together, they cannot give fruit. Trees are male and female. The female trees are fertilized by the male trees; they meet by the breeze of the wind. This is called pollination. In this connection, the birds and the bees may also be involved.

If a wife and husband do not meet, there is no child, and if two creepers do not meet together, there are no flowers or fruits. No one can be happy if they do not meet with another in love and affection.

Similarly, we can be connected to the Supreme Personality of Godhead by love and affection. We have love and affection now, but it is not transcendental. Now we become 'happy' by meat-eating, by taking drugs, by drinking alcohol, and so on.

Reporter: So you don't drink alcohol? Nothing?

Srila Gurudeva: No, never. That is why we are so happy now, and we will be happy forever.

Reporter: Unlike those of us who will get sclerosis of the liver.

Srila Gurudeva: If one is drinking alcohol and eating meat, he will be very cruel. Although he may be laughing and making merry, he may divorce his wife and also leave his children. However, those who have true love and affection in their heart – those who are chanting and remembering Krishna – they can conquer the entire world. Napoleon Bonaparte could not do so, and nor could Hitler. However, by love and affection, one can conquer the world – as we are doing. Everywhere I go, so many people come to me like little babies and children, and they follow

my words – because I have love and affection for
all. This is called *bhakti-yoga*. We have come here

By love and
affection, one can
conquer the
world.

to preach this mission of *bhakti-yoga*.

Do you have any other questions? Have you seen love?

Reporter: Have I seen love? I've never been in love.

Srila Gurudeva: What is love?

Reporter: Don't ask me. It hasn't happened to me yet.

Srila Gurudeva: I want to make you taste love; then you will be happy forever.

Reporter: I love my dogs.

Srila Gurudeva: But when these dogs will die... then?

Reporter: Then I will be very upset for a long time, and then I will go and get some more.

Srila Gurudeva: What will happen when those dogs are gone and you are also gone?

Reporter: I don't know. I am waiting for you to tell me that.

Srila Gurudeva: I have come to tell you that you

are coming from that eternal realm, and that is our abode, our eternal abode. "Back to Godhead, back to home" is our policy.

Reporter: That is what you are praying for?

Devotee: We are inviting everyone to come back to home, back to Godhead, and be happy forever.

Reporter: Now, in order to do that, this is the meditation? I read that from the age of 26 onwards, you vowed that you would chant 100,000 times a day?

Srila Gurudeva: When I was a student, I did not chant so much. I used to chant in the evening and morning. But when I became attached to Krishna, I would chant 100,000 names a day.

Reporter: What is it that you would chant 100,000 names?

Srila Gurudeva: *Hare Krishna, Hare Krishna, Krishna Krishna, Hare Hare, Hare Rama, Hare Rama, Rama Rama, Hare Hare.*

Reporter: 100,000 names?

Srila Gurudeva: Sometimes double that.

Reporter: How long does it take?

Srila Gurudeva: It may take more than 12 hours – continuous. Our Gurudeva and Srila Haridasa Thakura used to chant 300,000 names per day.

Reporter: What did they do – sleep, wake up, and then start chanting...?

Srila Gurudeva: No. They slept only 24 minutes throughout the day and night.

Reporter: 24 minutes of sleep? That's devotion, isn't it?! I need my sleep. So you do it 100,000 times each day? Some in the morning and some at night?

Srila Gurudeva: I wake up at about 3am in the morning and chant. Then I engage in reading and writing many books, giving classes here and there, and preaching up until 9pm at night. At 9pm I take some *prasadam* (foodstuffs offered to Sri Krishna) and then I go to bed.

Reporter: No food or drink at all during the day?

Interview by a Reporter

Srila Gurudeva: A little bit.

Reporter: Only a little?

Srila Gurudeva: Very little.

Reporter: This is very different than my lifestyle. You make me feel guilty. You have written 30 books, haven't you? Are they all original books or are they translations?

Srila Gurudeva: Mostly they are original, and some are translations.

Reporter: How many books have you sold?

Brajanath dasa: We have distributed about 100,000 [as of 1998] including Hindi publications and Internet downloading, and many of the devotees with Srila Gurudeva have distributed millions of books published by our *siksa-guru*, Srila Bhaktivedanta Swami Maharaja. Now he is publishing more and more books, which are being distributed as he travels around the world on his preaching tour.

Reporter: Are you working on a particular book

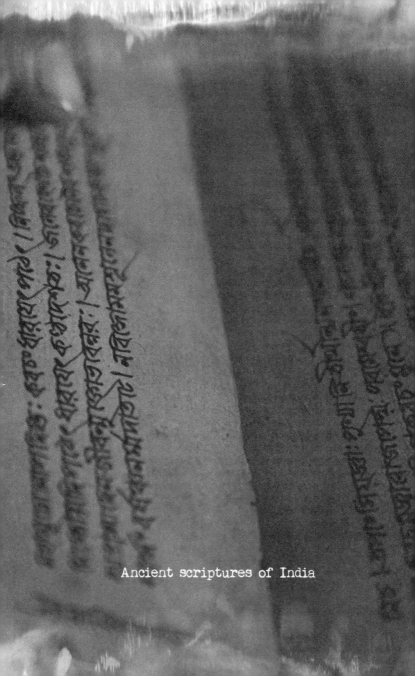
Ancient scriptures of India

at the moment?

Srila Gurudeva: Two books. There is a very good book in India called *Bhakti-rasamrta-sindhu*, meaning 'Ocean of Love and Affection', and another is called *Ujjvala-nilamani*.

Reporter: Translation?

Prema-prayojana dasa: 'The Effulgent Sapphire'. *Nilamani* means 'sapphire', and it refers to Krishna.

Reporter: I've never heard the word 'effulgent' before. I'll have to check it in my dictionary. When will these books be finished?

Srila Gurudeva: I think in 6 months. They are very big books. I have also translated and explained *Bhagavad-gita* in Hindi, and it is in the process of being translated in English. If you will come later, I will give you a copy.

Reporter: Now, the haircuts. I thought *my* haircut was short! All of my friends make fun of my short hair. So why is the hair of the men so short

and why the little ponytail?

Brajanath dasa: Why the shaven head and *sikha* (tuft of hair in the back of the shaven head, which remains uncut)?

Sripad Madhava Maharaja: A transcendental aerial.

[Devotees laughing…]

Srila Gurudeva: This is like a transcendental

aerial. By this *sikha* we can hear the transcendental words from the transcendental world, just as an antenna has some power to catch words.

Reporter (*laughing, speaking to Madhava Maharaja*): Oh, so you were serious. At first I thought that you were making fun of me.

Srila Gurudeva: No. What we are telling is true. It catches the sound. Just as an aerial catches sound, this *sikha* catches transcendental words. It is true to the highest extent. You know that the lines on our hands indicate something.

Reporter: Yes, I wrote an article on palmistry and had my palms read.

Srila Gurudeva: These lines are true, and this fact, which we are presenting now, is more true than that.

Reporter: A person's lines change according to what he does with his life.

Srila Gurudeva: There was a lady in India

whose son was on his way to England. When her son was in the channel between France and England, a heavy storm came and his boat was capsized. Water entered that boat from the bottom, and everyone in the boat was about to die. The son cried, "Oh Mother, oh Mother!" At that time, in Calcutta, India, his mother was thinking, "I wonder if there is some calamity befalling my son?" She quickly began to pray, "God, God, Krishna, Krishna!" After some time, by the grace of God, the son was saved. He later told his mother, "At that time I was calling, 'Mother, Mother!'" And his mother said, "At that same time, I was thinking there was some danger."

So, there is something in the heart. You have something there. If you pray to Krishna from your heart, Krishna will hear; God will hear. He will give you some transcendental news and inspire you. All our senses can be engaged by us in a way to connect us with Krishna, with God. All of our

Interview by a Reporter

"I am the syllable 'Om' in all Vedic mantras"

SRI KRISHNA IN BHAGAVAD-GITA

activities are in accordance with the injunctions of Vedic culture, and all these activities are very helpful for our meditation. We can change the lines on our palms by these *bhakti-yoga* activities, and we can also change our death-date.

Reporter: You will live longer? How is that?

Srila Gurudeva: Yes. It is written in scripture. There is proof. A man named Ajamila was dying, and he called out, '*Narayana! Narayana!*

Narayana!' which is one of the names of God. The date of his death was quickly postponed. After that, he chanted Krishna's name for 10 or 15 years, and after that his death was canceled.

Reporter: You mean he is still here?

Srila Gurudeva: He left the planet and his soul was liberated.

Reporter: So you're here from today, and you're giving speeches that are open to everybody?

Srila Gurudeva: Yes, we chant and remember Krishna, and give classes on *bhakti-yoga*. We do this to make everyone free from lust and anger. We can conquer lust, anger, and all other bodily urges very easily; and we can realize our soul and the controller of this world.

Do you know that God controls the waves of the sea? He controls the sun, so that it rises at a fixed time. Each minute passes, gradually reducing the duration of the day; and then a new, full day comes. All of the days are controlled by Him.

In our eyes, war has no value.

He is so merciful that if you call Him, He will hear you, He will nourish you, and He will give you the intelligence to know how you can meet Him.

Reporter: What about the usual questions about religion and God – like war and famine and that sort of thing?

Srila Gurudeva: Oh, in our eyes, war has no value.

Reporter: So why is it happening?

Srila Gurudeva: Wicked persons, who cannot control their senses, think, "I am the monarch of all." They like to quarrel with others and to

Those who have love and affection for all beings will quickly be liberated.

take others' property, praise, etc. They want to be happy, but they cannot be happy by this. Rather, Krishna arranges that they are destroyed by their wars. On the other hand, we know that no one has really died in war, because the soul is immortal. This body is mortal, but the soul is immortal.

Reporter: Oh, I see.

Srila Gurudeva: We are not so worried about these things. War has been going on from the beginning of this creation, and all beings are traveling in the endless cycle of birth and death. Those who do not remember Krishna, God, will have to come and take birth again, and they will suffer.

However, those who are chanting, remembering, and performing spiritual pious activities, knowing that all beings in this world are like children separated from their father, they are sons of God, all are like brothers and sisters, they will not suffer. Rather, those who have love and affection for all beings will quickly be liberated. They will go to Krishna and will never come back to this world. As for others, they are bound to come and fight with each other, and to die and again take birth. It may be that they will come in the species of animals such as hogs and pigs.

Reporter: Oh, that's like you become a worm if you did something terrible before, isn't it? You put it in very simple words.

Where will you go after Perth?

Srila Gurudeva: From here we will go to Brisbane, then to Fiji, Melbourne, Singapore, again Melbourne and Sydney, from there to the Philippines, and then India.

Reporter: Very nice.

Srila Gurudeva: On the next tour we will go to Hawaii, Canada, France, Germany, Italy, and many other places. You can travel with us here and there. I am happy to meet you. This was a very pleasant talk.

Hare Krishna

"Love existed at the beginning of the universe. Love is really our religion, our eternal dharma."

SAT-SANGA DISCOURSE

SEPTEMBER 22, 2002

. 6 .

The Philosophy of Love

The Philosophy of Love

I want to give you a general idea of *Srimad-Bhagavatam*. It is stated by Srila Krishna Dvaipayana Vyasa, who is one of the incarnations of Krishna, that the Supreme Lord created this world. He is very powerful, and that is why He is called God; G stands for 'Generator or creator', O for 'Operator or manager', and D stands for 'Destroyer'.

Our Vedic sages, like Vyasadeva, Narada, and Brahma, have told us that the Supreme Lord has a very beautiful form and many millions of transcendental qualities. If a father has a form, then only may his son have a form. If the father has no form or qualities, the son will neither have form nor qualities, nor can He even exist. It is stated in our scriptures:

aho bhāgyam aho bhāgyaṁ
nanda-gopa-vrajaukasām
yan-mitraṁ paramānandaṁ
pūrṇaṁ brahma sanātanam

"How greatly fortunate are Nanda Maharaja, the cowherd men and all the other inhabitants of Vrindavan! There is no limit to their good fortune, because the Absolute Truth, the source of transcendental bliss, the eternal Supreme Brahman, has become their friend."

Srimad-Bhagavatam (10.14.32)

Lord Sri Krishna, the son of Nanda Baba in Vraja, is very beautiful, sweet, and merciful. He sports with His cowherd boys and millions of *gopis* – dancing, singing, making merry, and playing on His flute. He is not an ordinary person; He is the Lord of lords. He is *purna-brahma sanatana*, unlimited and unparalleled. No one is equal to Him and no one can be greater than Him; all are subordinate to Him. He does not directly create these worlds. The servants of the servants of His servants create them all, whereas He Himself is always engaged in playing and giving pleasure to all His associates.

A shadow of this truth has been explained in the Bible, wherein it is said, "God created man after His own image" – this is the same thing. The Supreme Lord has created man. He is beautiful and He also made man like that. In the Bible it has been written that the Supreme Lord has a form. It has also been written in the Koran of the Muslims and in other religious scriptures that Allah created man in His own image. No one can deny these statements of the Bible and the Koran.

Jesus went to India when he was about sixteen years old, and he visited many places of pilgrimage, like Vrindavan, Ayodhya, South India, and Jagannatha Puri. In Puri he saw Jagannatha, Baladeva and Subhadra, and he heard Lord Jagannatha addressed as Krishna. From this name came Krushna, then Krushta, then Krishta, and then Christ – Krishna and Christ – the name is the same. There are no separate Gods.

In this entire universe there is only one Supreme God. There are many conceptions

Our eyes can speak the language of love... a smiling face can tell everything.

of God, but the Supreme God is not Russian, British, German, or Australian. He knows all languages perfectly, and ultimately there is no need of knowing these languages. There is only one real language in the entire world, and that language is called love.

Our eyes can speak the language of love, our ears and our hands can speak and understand the language of love, and a smiling face can tell everything. Our Supreme Lord Krishna knows all languages with no difficulty. God is one and He is Krishna. All other names, like Brahma,

Paramatma, Buddha, Allah, and God are included within Him.

Krishna is love, and His love is Radhika. Without love – without Radhika – He cannot exist for even a second. If you want to meet Krishna, in a moment you can do so if you follow Radhika and call out to Her, "O Radhika!" Krishna will then come at once.

This is the philosophy of love, and it is imperative that we know this philosophy.

Srimad-Bhagavatam is the philosophy of love, *Sri Caitanya-caritamrita* is the essence of love, and the books of Srila Rupa Gosvami, such as *Ujjvala Nilamani* and others, are all about transcendental love and nothing else. For example, in the first verse of the *Srimad-Bhagavatam*, Srila Vyasadeva and Srila Sukadeva Gosvami offer obeisances to the Supreme Lord:

The Philosophy of Love

oṁ namo bhagavate vāsudevāya

janmādy asya yato 'nvayād itarataś

cārtheṣv abhijñaḥ svarāṭ

tene brahma hṛdā ya ādi-kavaye

muhyanti yat sūrayaḥ

tejo-vāri-mṛdāṁ yathā vinimayo

yatra tri-sargo 'mṛṣā

dhāmnā svena sadā nirasta-kuhakaṁ

satyaṁ paraṁ dhīmahi

"O my Lord, Sri Krishna, son of Vasudeva, O all-pervading Personality of Godhead, I offer my respectful obeisances unto You. I meditate upon Lord Sri Krishna because He is the Absolute Truth and the primeval cause of all causes of the creation, sustenance and destruction of the manifested universes. He is directly and indirectly conscious of all manifestations, and He is independent because there is no other cause beyond Him. It is He only who first imparted the Vedic

Sri Brahmaji

knowledge unto the heart of Brahmaji, the first
created being. By Him even the great sages and
demigods are placed into illusion, as one is be-
wildered by the illusory representations of water
seen in fire, or land seen on water. Only because
of Him do the material universes, temporarily

manifested by the reactions of the three modes of nature, appear factual, although they are unreal. I therefore meditate upon Him, Lord Sri Krishna, who is eternally existent in the transcendental abode, which is forever free from the illusory representations of the material world. I meditate upon Him, for He is the Absolute Truth." *Srimad-Bhagavatam* (1.1.1)

Although Srila Vyasadeva is addressing Krishna in this way: "You are creating this world; You are the supreme cause of this creation", he knows that this is a secondary consideration. It is not primary. Krishna can at once create millions and millions of universes simply by His eyes or by His wish.

Krishna is fully independent. No one can control Him and there are none equal to Him. Even Lord Brahma, the creator of this universe, can understand something about Krishna in his meditation, but he does not understand Him

THE DIVINE COUPLE

Srimati Radhika & Sri Krishna

fully. He does not know who He is and how He performs all of His wondrous feats. Krishna has a very powerful energy; and this energy is called Radhika and sometimes Yogamaya. He also has His shadow, the illusory *maya*, and by the work of this shadow energy we sometimes imagine we are seeing water in earth and fire in water.

The meaning here is that this body is mortal. It is made of stool, urine, blood and many other foul substances. Although this is a fact, still we think, "I am this body, this world is true, and it is mine." This is the influence of Krishna's deluding potency called *maya-shakti*. I have come only to point this out and to encourage you to be careful in this regard.

In this world there is no pure love and affection. The appearance of love and affection here is also due to Krishna's deluding potency called *maya*. In this world we have great affection for our wives and our children, but that blind love is not pure. If your wife is very beautiful, energetic, and always serving you, you keep her; but if she becomes invalid in any way and not so beautiful, you will change your wife. You will divorce her and get a new wife. In the same way, a lady also gives up her husband if he is not doing well and is not serving her. Thus, there is only conditional love and affection in this world; it is not real. We cannot love anyone by these bodies. The only pure love is experienced by the soul for the Supersoul. It is for this reason – to give you this pure love – that we have come to you.

Due to the deluding *maya*, we misunderstand this world to be true and our affection to be true, but it is actually extremely painful. Becoming old and dying is very painful. You cannot take with you what you are collecting day and night in this world. Moreover, you cannot take your body and present mental conceptions with you. Therefore, what is the use of laboring like donkeys? There is

Sri Sri Radha Krishna

TRANSCENDENTAL TRUTH

no need to do so.

We are offering our prostrated obeisances, Srila Vyasadeva is offering his prostrated obeisances, and Srila Sukadeva Gosvami is offering his prostrated obeisances, to He whose deluding potency *maya* makes us blind and ignorant.

In the first verse, Srila Vyasadeva has stated, "*satyam param dhimahi*. I meditate on *parama-satyam* (the transcendental truth), Srimati Radhika with Krishna." Offering respectful obeisances and meditating in this way is the essence of the first verse. In the second verse of the *Srimad-Bhagavatam*, Sri Vyasadeva again offers His respectful obeisances:

> *dharmaḥ projjhita-kaitavo 'tra*
> *paramo nirmatsarāṇāṁ satāṁ*
> *vedyaṁ vāstavam atra vastu śivadaṁ*
> *tāpa-trayonmūlanam*
> *śrīmad-bhāgavate mahā-muni-kṛte*
> *kiṁ vā parair īśvaraḥ*
> *sadyo hṛdy avarudhyate 'tra*
> *kṛtibhiḥ śuśrūṣubhis tat-kṣaṇāt*

"Completely rejecting all religious activities which are materially motivated, this *Bhagavata Purana* propounds the highest truth, which is understandable by those devotees who are fully pure in heart. The highest truth is reality distinguished from illusion for the welfare of all.

The Philosophy of Love

Such truth uproots the threefold miseries. This beautiful *Bhagavatam*, compiled by the great sage Vyasadeva [in his maturity], is sufficient in itself for God realization. What is the need of any other scripture? As soon as one attentively and submissively hears the message of *Bhagavatam*, by this culture of knowledge the Supreme Lord is established within his heart".

In this world there are many kinds of new religions, although they are actually not religions. They are not eternal religions. These religions (dharmas), can only give us information about how to maintain our worldly lives. The adherents of Buddha-dharma, for example, do not discuss any relation with the Supreme Lord; they only consider their relationship with mortal bodies, and it is therefore not eternal. Nowadays, Buddha-dharma is everywhere, but its followers do not believe in the Vedas. Actually, it is not religion. Its followers do not believe in God and in fact they do not believe in anything. They do not even believe in their own existence, and they accept nothing more than false logic. If someone will follow them, he may lose his existence – in the sense that he will merge with the impersonal *brahma*, where there is no activity, no form, and no qualities. This is likened to losing one's existence or becoming zero. Buddha-dharma is pervading everywhere, like the air, so beware of it.

If the world is false, if God is false, if we are false, then love is also false. Without love, however, we cannot maintain our lives for even a

Love is really our religion, and this love is our eternal, Vedic dharma.

The Philosophy of Love

Nowadays, Buddha-dharma is everywhere, but
its followers do not believe in the Vedas.

second, and therefore their theory is totally false.
Whereas they advocate no love at all, our God is
supreme, eternal, and He is the embodiment of
love and affection.

Do you know what religion was in this world
earlier than 2002 years ago? Christianity is only
2002 years old, and younger than that is the

Muslim faith, which is only 1400 years old. But love existed at the beginning of the universe. Love is really our religion, and this love is called Sanatana (eternal) dharma, or Vedic dharma.

If you throw a piece of stone, earth, wood, or any other solid or liquid object in the sky, it will go upward and then return down. Why? This is due to the Earth's law of gravitation. Anything made of earth, wood, and so on will fall down if there is nothing to hold it up.

On the other hand, flames of a fire also go up, but they do not turn again towards the earth. If you send a balloon into the sky, it will go up and it may be that it will never return. The example of the balloon is given because a balloon refers to the air, and air and fire are not part of the earth. When any part of a whole meets with its whole, the two will exist together in harmony. Otherwise, if they do not have this relationship, they will not. Similarly, we are part and parcel of the

The Philosophy of Love

Supreme Lord, so unless we meet Him with love and affection, we cannot be happy. This is the philosophy of love.

Even dangerous lions, tigers, bears, and very poisonous snakes, and even dacoits, have some kind of love. Despite our repeated change of body, only love will remain with us. We all want happiness, and real happiness is nothing but love.

Does anyone present here want to suffer? You can raise your hands if you want suffering, and I will give it to you at once. Nobody likes suffering. All want happiness, and this happiness is pure love.

But love does not mean body-to-body. Inside the body is the soul and the Supersoul, Krishna. The Supreme Lord is also there. He is everywhere, and if we attain pure love and affection for Him, then we can serve Him eternally – and He can be controlled. This is the philosophy of the *Srimad-Bhagavatam*.

The Supreme Lord is very kind; He is cause-lessly merciful. He has given us a very valu-able asset, and that asset is love. We have love, but we will have to purify it by loving Krishna. Only in this way will He be controlled. The only way to be happy, and the only way to control the Supreme Lord, is by this love and affection that He has personally donated to us.

The philosophy of love has been given in the *Srimad-Bhagavatam*, and therefore *Srimad-Bhagavatam* not only gives philosophy, but also examples of real love and affection. It ex-plains how the *gopis* (cowherd damsels) and other *Vraja-vasis* (residents of Vrindavan) love Krishna fully, with their lives and souls. If one hears *Srimad-Bhagavatam* and thinks about even one line or even half of a line, or even one word – Krishna or Radha – he will attain that pure love and be able to control the Supreme Lord.

Sri Vyasadeva, in his trance of meditation,

The Philosophy of Love

We have come from that eternal realm, our eternal home.

realized the full love felt between Krishna and all His associates. He also saw how a conditioned soul forgets Krishna and falls down to this material world, and how one who remembers His names attains that love and affection very quickly. We should try to hear very carefully and attentively whatever *Srimad-Bhagavatam* is telling us.

The transcendental religion explained in *Srimad-Bhagavatam* is not periodical or partial. It is not like worldly intoxication in the name of religion. Rather, it is permanent transcendental love and affection. If anyone will hear it, he will be happy in this life and, giving up his body, his pure soul will go to Goloka Vrindavan (Krishna's supreme abode) and he will be happy there.

It is true that we are not seeing Krishna, but He sees us, and He may hear what we say to Him. We do not hear what He is telling us, and we do not hear His calling us by playing His flute, but our call is heard by Krishna, who is very kind and causelessly merciful. He has sent all our *guru-parampara acaryas* (spiritual teachers in disciplic succession), He has also sent Jesus, and sometimes He Himself descends with all His associates – only because He loves us.

He is calling us: "Come, come - My sons and daughters! Chant this mantra: *Hare Krishna, Hare Krishna, Krishna Krishna, Hare Hare — Hare Rama, Hare Rama, Rama Rama, Hare Hare.*

Chant even one time. I will take you to Goloka Vrindavan and you will be transcendentally happy forever." Do not be hopeless; never be hopeless. You can always have hope, because He is weeping for us. He is lamenting for us.

We cannot lament or weep for Him, but He is lamenting and weeping for us. Go on chanting, remembering and offering obeisances, and you will be able to very quickly attain all the invaluable gifts I have described.

Gaura Premanande! Hari Haribol!

CALL OUT THE NAMES OF LORD HARI
IN GREAT BLISS AND LOVE

"His heart brimmed with the most profound realizations of Radha and Krishna's pastimes…"

FIRST PUBLISHED IN

"THE RAYS OF THE HARMONIST"

N⁰. 23, VYASA-PUJA EDITION

· 7 ·

A Glimpse Into Gurudeva's Life

SRI SRIMAD BHAKTIVEDANTA
NARAYANA GOSVAMI MAHARAJA

A Glimpse Into Gurudeva's Life

On the new moon day of the month of Magha (February) 1921, Sri Srimad Bhaktivedanta Narayana Gosvami Maharaja took his divine birth in a highly educated and respected *brahmana* (priestly) family in the village of Tiwaripura, in the Buxar district of Bihar, India. He was given the name Sriman Narayana. His parents were devout Vaisnava devotees of the Lord, and from the time he was a small baby, Sriman Narayana was regularly taken by his father to recitations of the Ramayana epic, which he grew to love.

In February 1946, he met his *gurudeva*, Sri Srimad Bhakti Prajnana Keshava Gosvami Maharaja, and his life of complete and exemplary dedication to his *gurudeva* began. Upon taking *harinama* and *diksha* initiation from him, he received the name 'Sri Gaura Narayana'. He accompanied his *gurudeva* on his extensive preaching

A Glimpse Into Gurudeva's Life

Sri Srimad Bhakti Prajñana Keshava Gosvami Maharaja
(1898-1968)

tours throughout India, rendering him personal service and also actively assisting him in preaching. This included regularly hosting the thousands of pilgrims attending the yearly Navadvipa-dhama *parikrama* and Vraja-mandala *parikrama* festivals, which years later, still draw thousands of devotees from the world over.

Sri Gaura Narayana was known for his respectful and affectionate dealings with all Vaisnavas, in particular with his two God-brothers, Sri Sajjana-sevaka Brahmacari and Sri Radha-natha dasa[1]. These three stalwart Vaisnavas of the highest calibre assumed responsibility for their *gurudeva*'s mission in a mood of harmony and co-operation that would last the duration of their lives. In 1952, all three were given the renounced order, and Sri Gaura Narayana became Sri Bhaktivedanta Narayana Gosvami Maharaja. In his early *matha* (monastery) life, he met Sri Srimad Bhaktivedanta Swami Maharaja, the world famous preacher of Gaudiya Vaisnavism. In the future, he would render superlative service to Sri Srimad Bhaktivedanta Swami Maharaja by nurturing the tender seeds of *bhakti* in the hearts of so many of his dear

---

1   Sri Sajjana-sevaka Brahmacari and Sri Radhanatha
     dasa were given the names Sri Bhaktivedanta Vamana
     Gosvami Maharaja and Sri Bhaktivedanta Trivikrama
     Gosvami Maharaja, respectively.

disciples and followers around the globe.

In 1954 Sri Srimad Bhaktivedanta Narayana Gosvami Maharaja was given responsibility for Sri Kesavaji Gaudiya Matha in Mathura. Under him, the *matha* flourished, as the local residents of Vraja came to experience the consummate care of one who is truly an eternal resident of Vraja. His *gurudeva* had instructed him to translate the writings of prominent Gaudiya Vaisnavas into Hindi, a task he assiduously assumed throughout his entire life and which resulted in the publication of nearly fifty Hindi texts. These invaluable masterpieces are currently being translated into the major languages of the world.

Since his heart brimmed with the most profound realizations of Radha and Krishna's pastimes, which automatically include all philosophical truths, it was radiant with the deepest affection. Those who heard his *hari-katha* (sacred narrations and philosophical discourses)

felt supreme protection from the onslaught of material miseries and experienced a deeper commitment to the path of *bhakti*. When he uttered the Hare Krishna *maha-mantra* at the time of initiation, it bore the same effect. He is famous throughout Vraja-mandala and the entire world for how he transformed people's hearts in these ways.

For many years, he traveled throughout India to spread the message of Gaudiya Vaisnavism. In the mid 1980s, the first Western devotees

His heart brimmed with the most profound realizations of Radha and Krishna's pastimes...

came to receive his guidance, and in 1996, at the repeated request of the Western devotees, he went to Europe and America. During the next fourteen years, he circled the globe more than thirty times. Whether he was in India or abroad, his preaching always bore the distinctive characteristic of boldly unmasking any misconception obscuring the specific purposes of Sriman Mahaprabhu's advent, in strict adherence to the desire of Srila Bhaktisiddhanta Sarasvati Thakura Prabhupada and in perfect congruence with the conceptions of Srila Rupa Gosvami. Thus, in

SRI CAITANYA MAHAPRABHU

upholding the glorious tenets of the *sampradaya* (spiritual lineage), he performed the function of a true *acarya* (teacher who leads by example).

A most endearing hallmark of his preaching was the heart-melting affection he showed to all. As an *uttama-bhagavata* (pure devotee of the Lord), he entered the deepest recesses of the heart to give the unmistakable reassurance that he was one's eternal well-wisher. The depth of his affection is a tangible reality for all who have experienced it, and this in itself bears subjective testimony to the fact that he was a true emissary of the Supreme Lord. As thousands of devotees will affirm, his genuine interest in the spiritual well-being of all souls was evident in his equal love and affection for all. He cared not if a person were his disciple, the disciple of another, or of another philosophical school altogether. His divine affection knew no bounds.

At the age of almost ninety years old, on December 29th 2010, at 3.00 am, at Cakra Tirtha, Sri Jagannatha Puri-dhama in the state of Orissa, India, he concluded his pastimes in this world. That day was the sacred appearance day of his beloved Godbrother, *nitya-lila pravista om visnupada* Sri Srimad Bhaktivedanta Vamana Gosvami Maharaja. The following day, in Sri Navadvipa-dhama, Sri Gaura-sundara's fully empowered emissary, the very embodiment of His unique compassion, was given *samadhi* (sacred funeral rites). He will never cease to reside in his divine instructions and in the hearts of those who are devoted to him. He used to say, "Do not think that I will ever leave you – never, ever. I am always with you."

In a mood of insignificance and longing for his mercy, we fall at his lotus feet and pray that he bless our attempts to always be able to render him some service.

Aspiring to serve Sri Guru and the Vaisnavas,
The Rays of The Harmonist team

A Glimpse Into Gurudeva's Life

The temple in Jagannatha Puri

First published in The Rays of The Harmonist:
"A Glimpse of the Life of *nitya-lila pravista om visnupada* Sri Srimad Bhaktivedanta Narayana Gosvami Maharaja"

Nº 23, Vyasa-puja Edition, Mauni Amavasya 2011

WWW.RAYSOFTHEHARMONIST.COM

My contribution to the present and future generation of devotees is largely embodied in the books that I am writing and translating. They are my legacy.

Srila Bhaktivedanta Narayana Gosvami Maharaja founded Gaudiya Vedanta Publications to publish his translations of the books of the previous Vaishnava acaryas (self-realized teachers) in English, Hindi, Bengali, Spanish, and many other languages and has globally distributed millions of these books. The GVP Archive offers an extensive audio and video collection of classes on the teachings in these books, and is dedicated to ensure their availability to audiences worldwide.

GAUDIYA VEDANTA PUBLICATIONS

Gaudiya Vedanta Publications (GVP) is a non-profit publishing group, dedicated to preserving, publishing, and propagating the authentic bhakti yoga teachings of Gaudiya Vaisnavism as taught and demonstrated by one of the most notable proponents of the bhakti tradition, philosophy and practice of our time, Srila Bhaktivedanta Narayana Gosvami Maharaja.

INTERNATIONAL
PURE BHAKTI YOGA SOCIETY

*The International Pure Bhakti Yoga Society
is dedicated to cultivating and nourishing the eternal,
essential nature of all living beings (jaiva-dharma),
irrespective of caste, creed, or color, by making
available the spiritual teachings of the ancient Vedas,
arising from India's cradle of Wisdom, accompanied
by association with self-realized souls through
gatherings (sat-sanga), study courses
and immersion programs.*

*We invite you to attend our programs and
experience a scriptural narration, ecstatic kirtan
(sacred chanting), and mantra meditation at
one of our locations worldwide.*

ipbys.com